What Makes an Animal an Animal?

by Gary Rushworth

Table of Contents

Pictures To Think About

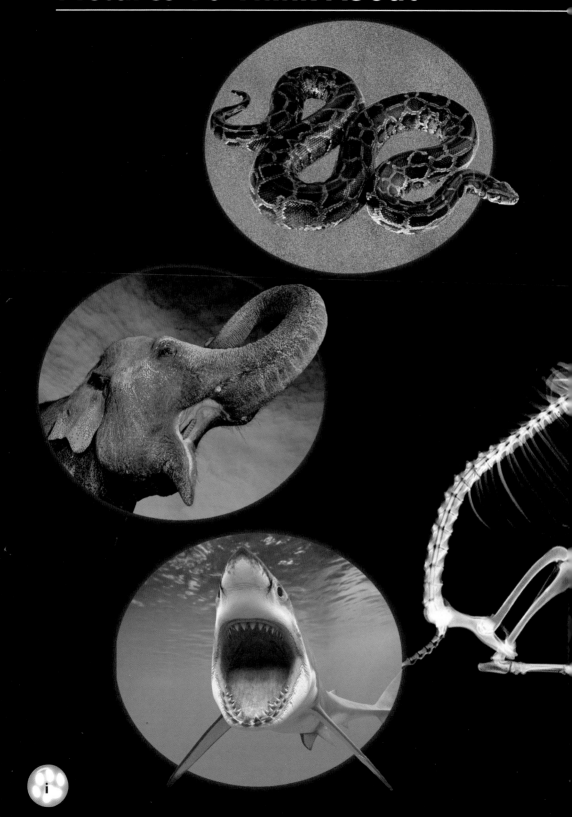

Words To Think About

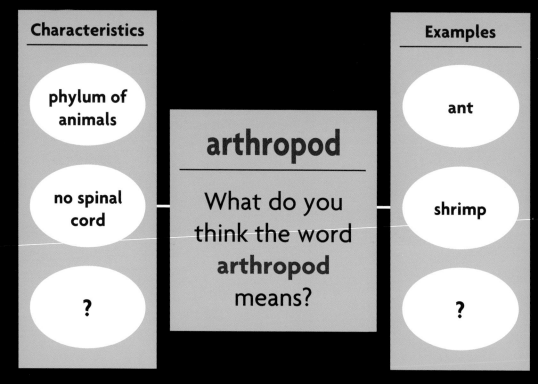

Characteristics

phylum of animals

no spinal cord

?

arthropod

What do you think the word **arthropod** means?

Examples

ant

shrimp

?

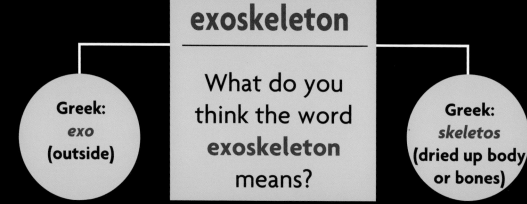

exoskeleton

What do you think the word **exoskeleton** means?

Greek:
exo
(outside)

Greek:
skeletos
(dried up body or bones)

Read for More Clues

arthropod,   page 7
class,   page 9
exoskeleton, page 7

class

What do you think the word **class** means in this book?

Meaning 1
group of students taught in the same room (noun)

Meaning 2
group of living things between phylum and order that share traits (noun)

Meaning 3
rank or rating based on quality (noun)

Introduction

How many animals can you name? Ten? Fifty? One hundred? Earth has more than one million types of animals. How do we keep track of them all? To keep track, scientists sort animals into groups. Scientists have special groups for all living things.

How do scientists sort living things? Scientists study how living things are alike. They look at what living things are made of. They look at what living things eat. They look at how living things reproduce. They also look at how living things feed their young.

There are so many ▶ animals that it is hard to keep track of them all.

This book is all about animals. You will see how animals are alike. You will see how they are different. You will learn how they have changed over time.

Animals are in one large group. People belong to the same group. Read on. Learn what makes an animal an animal.

▼ People are in the same large group as the buffalo.

Classification of Living Things

All living things have features, or **traits** (TRAYTS). Living things with the same traits are put in the same groups. Each living thing is then given a name. The names are Latin and Greek words. This system is called **classification** (kla-sih-fih-KAY-shun). How does classification work?

Careers

Taxonomist

The science of classifying organisms is called taxonomy. Taxonomists are scientists who study how organisms are alike and then group the organisms by their similarities.

They Made a Difference

Aristotle (384–322 B.C.) was a Greek philosopher and scientist. He was the first person to separate plants and animals into groups.

Scientists sort animals into smaller and smaller groups. The groups are based on shared traits. Look at the chart below. The animals near the top of the chart are in bigger groups. These animals have little in common. Further down the chart, the groups get smaller. These animals are more and more alike.

Everyday Science

skunk

Classification Chart

Kingdom

Phylum

Class

Order

Family

Genus

Species

beetle

dog

The Kingdom

Kingdoms (KING-dumz) are the largest groups of living things. All plants are in the plant kingdom. All animals are in the animal kingdom. There are five kingdoms in all.

Members of the animal kingdom can move. Unlike plants, animals do not make their own food. They eat other living things.

Everyday Science

Kingdoms

Animalia

Plantae

Fungi

Protista

Monera

Scientists separate organisms into five kingdoms. Each kingdom includes organisms that are alike and have common ancestors.

The Phylum

Kingdoms have smaller groups called **phyla** (FY-luh). The animal kingdom has three main phyla. One phylum is **chordates** (KOR-dates).

Another phylum of animals is **arthropods** (AR-thruh-podz). Arthropods have hard skeletons outside their bodies. These skeletons are **exoskeletons** (ek-soh-SKEH-leh-tunz). Arthropods have bodies with many joints, or segments. Most insects are arthropods.

Chordates are animals that have a spinal cord. The spinal cord of some chordates is wrapped in bone. The spinal cord and bone form a backbone. Chordates with backbones are **vertebrates** (VER-teh-bruts).

A few chordates do not have backbones. These chordates are **invertebrates** (in-VER-teh-bruts).

Solve This

1. Invertebrate animals make up over 97% of the animal kingdom. What percentage of animals are vertebrates?

✔ Point

How can you check your answer?

▼ A dog is a vertebrate.

▲ protozoa

Each phylum has smaller groups called **classes**. All birds are in the same class. Birds have feathers. Animals that feed milk to their young are in another class. This class is mammals. Humans are mammals.

Orders come after classes. Primates are one order. Primates are animals with obvious hands and feet. They also have short noses and large brains.

classification ▶ chart for a rhesus monkey

Rhesus Monkey

Kingdom	Animalia
Phylum	Chordata
Class	Mammalia
Order	Primates
Family	Cercopithecidae
Genus	Macaca
Species	*Macaca mulatta*

Solve This

2. A rhesus monkey feeds its young with milk from its body. Determine what class this animal belongs to.

✔ **Point**

What do all these animals have in common?

9

Orders have smaller groups called **families**. For example, the Primate order has a family called Hominidae. This family includes humans, gorillas, and chimpanzees.

Genus (JEE-nus) is the next smallest group. Foxes, wolves, and dogs belong to the same family. Only wolves and dogs are in the same genus. Foxes are in a different genus. **Species** (SPEE-sheez) is the smallest group of all.

It's a Fact The term Hominidae means "Great Ape."

A collie, a poodle, and a German shepherd are in the same genus. They are all dogs. But each of those dogs is a different species.

✔ **Point**

Talk About It
Ask several classmates to describe their favorite dogs. Together, create a species chart comparing the dogs by size, physical features, and personality traits.

Great Dane

The Great Dane ▶ and Papillon are two different species of dog.

Papillon

11

What Makes Animals Different?

One trait of animals is how they can move. Think of your favorite animal. How does this animal move? Does it fly? Does it swim? Does it walk and run? Perhaps it can do all of these things.

Some animals walk on two legs. Some animals walk on four legs. Some animals slither or crawl.

Scientists believe that the first animals lived in the sea. These animals were aquatic, or water, animals. The first land animals lived millions of years later.

The first living things had only one cell. Over time, animals evolved, or formed, from these single cells. Some early animals died. Others changed into the animals we know today.

Solve This

3. The first sea animals are believed to have developed 550 million years ago. The first land animals are believed to have developed 530 million years ago. How many millions of years after the aquatic animals developed did the terrestrial animals appear?

✔ Point

What steps did you take to get your answer?

◀ Life began in the oceans.

Animals of Yesterday

Dakosaurus (DAK-oh-sor-us) was an early sea animal. This animal is related to the crocodile.

Dinocephalosaurus (die-noh-SEF-uh-luh-sor-us) was another early sea animal. It was a lot like a dinosaur (DIE-nuh-sor). This animal lived around 230 million years ago. It used its long neck to capture food.

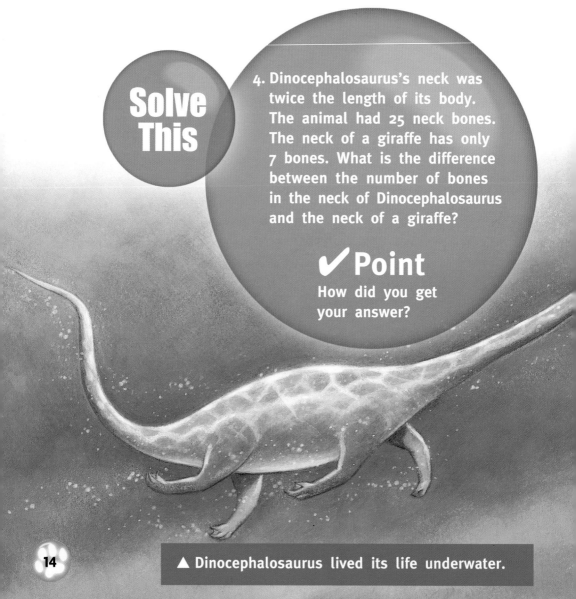

Solve This

4. Dinocephalosaurus's neck was twice the length of its body. The animal had 25 neck bones. The neck of a giraffe has only 7 bones. What is the difference between the number of bones in the neck of Dinocephalosaurus and the neck of a giraffe?

✔ **Point**

How did you get your answer?

▲ Dinocephalosaurus lived its life underwater.

Over time, many early dinosaurs began to **adapt** (uh-DAPT) to life on land. To adapt means to change. These animals developed strong legs. They could find new foods. Dinosaurs soon lived all over the world.

Around 150 million years ago, animals began to fly. The first flying animals were part reptile and part bird. These animals had beaks like birds. They also had a full set of teeth.

This animal was 13 feet (4 meters) ▼ long. Its jaw was 2 feet (.6 meters) long, with 4-inch (10-centimeter) teeth.

▲ Dinosaurs lived during the Mesozoic period, which lasted about 150 million years.

Animals Today

Look around you. How many different animals can you see? Remember, Earth has more than one million different types of animals.

Many animals live in the sea. But they are not all fish. The largest known sea animal is the blue whale. The blue whale is a mammal.

It's a Fact

The blue whale lives on a diet of small fish, plankton, and tiny shrimp-like creatures called krill. A blue whale eats about 8,000 pounds (3,629 kilograms) of food each day.

The blue whale is the ▲ largest animal ever to have lived on Earth.

Great white sharks have been around for thousands of years. The great white is related to the Megalodon (MEG-uh-loh-don). This fish lived thousands of years ago. This fish was just like the great white shark, except for one thing. The Megalodon was three times as big as the great white!

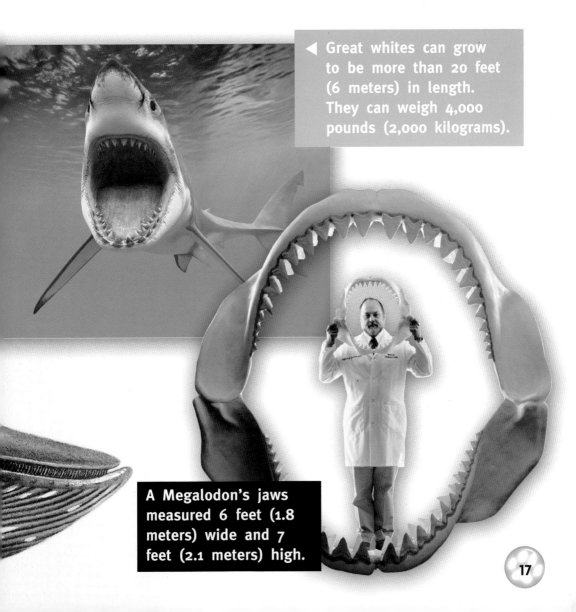

◀ Great whites can grow to be more than 20 feet (6 meters) in length. They can weigh 4,000 pounds (2,000 kilograms).

A Megalodon's jaws measured 6 feet (1.8 meters) wide and 7 feet (2.1 meters) high.

What Do Animals Need to Survive?

Animals have changed over time. Why do some species survive, or stay alive? Why do other species die out? We know some reasons why. All animals need basic things to survive. All animals need food and water to live. They also need a place to raise their young. Sometimes, nature causes a species to die out. Sometimes, humans are to blame.

▲ The earliest reptiles overcame many obstacles to survive.

All animals need a habitat. A habitat is where an animal lives. Habitats provide the food, water, and shelter animals need.

Animals must adapt to their habitats. They may change the food they eat. Their bodies may change to help them live in cold places. These changes are called **adaptations** (a-dap-TAY-shunz). Adaptations help animals survive.

▼ Animals are dependent upon their habitats for survival.

▲ Animals adapted to their environments are more likely to survive.

Adaptations take many forms. The shape of a bird's beak is an adaptation. Sharp teeth are an adaptation. The long trunk of an elephant is also an adaptation.

The ways of animals may also change. For example, an animal may begin to live high up in trees. This protects it from other animals.

▼ When attacked, grazing animals usually scatter in different directions, confusing the attacker.

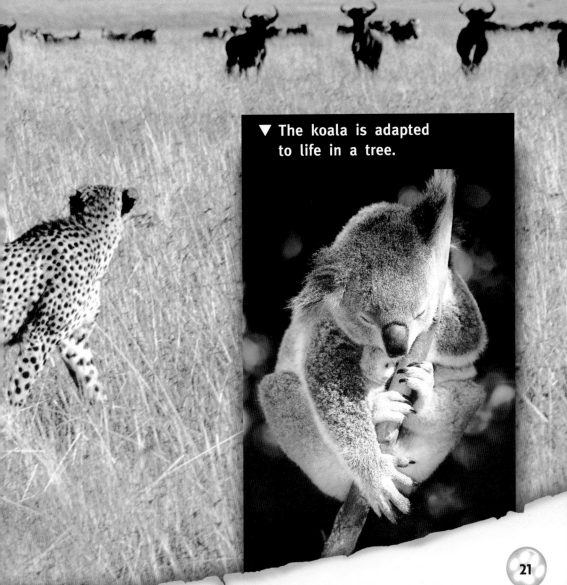

▼ The koala is adapted to life in a tree.

Some animals use bad smells to scare away other animals. Some animals use **camouflage** (KA-muh-flahj) to hide. Their covering blends into their surroundings.

Fish use heavy sea grass to hide from predators. ▼

▲ Skunks use a foul-smelling chemical spray to avoid being attacked.

◄ The praying mantis uses camouflage to blend in with its surroundings.

Many animals use scent and camouflage to hunt. Some animals make toxins, or poisons. Toxins make other animals sick.

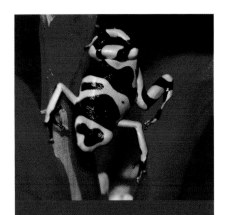

▲ The poison dart frog produces a toxin that can be deadly.

▲ A leopard's spots allow it to hide.

23

When habitats change, animals must adapt. If animals cannot adapt, they die out.

Habitats change easily. Animals can adapt to small things, like the changing seasons. If food and water run low, many animals move away. Then they move back later.

▼ Habitats are easily lost and destroyed.

Sometimes, animals cannot adapt. People clear land to build roads and houses. Clearing land takes away habitats. The animals may not come back.

Too many animals can be bad for a habitat. Taking away animals can also hurt. All living things are part of the food chain. Taking away one part of the food chain can harm other animals. Habitats must be kept in balance.

Extinction

An animal goes extinct (ik-STINGKT) when the last of its kind dies. Some animals are close to going extinct. They are endangered (in-DANE-jerd).

How can we stop extinction? One way is to protect habitats. Another way is to protect species. Sea otters were hunted for their fur. They became endangered. Now, laws protect them from hunters.

▲ The sea otter remains on the endangered list.

American bison live in North America. Millions of bison once roamed the plains. In the 1800s, the bison were hunted. The species almost went extinct. Then laws were made to protect the bison. Today, hundreds of thousands of bison roam free.

Many great birds are endangered, too. Hunting and loss of habitat are the reasons. Today, the bald eagle is protected. The California condor is also protected. Their numbers are growing again.

◀ The bald eagle nearly became extinct.

The California condor is a protected species. ▶

27

Conclusion

Earth has more than one million types of animals. Scientists use a system to keep track of them all. This system is called classification.

Classification helps people study animals. Classification shows how animals are alike. It also shows how they are different.

The more we know about animals, the more we can do to protect animals and their habitats.

✔ Point

Read More About It
You've read about many types of animals. To learn more, ask your teacher or librarian to help you find books, magazines, and Internet sites about the animal or group of animals you find most interesting.

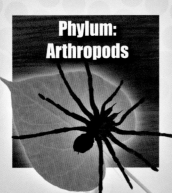

Phylum: Arthropods

Class: Mammalia

Order: Primate

Animal Kingdom

Family: Hominidae

Genus: Canis

Species: Great White Shark

Solve This Answers

1. Page 8 3%
   100 − 97 = 3
2. Page 9 mammalia
3. Page 13 20 million years
   550 million − 530 million = 20 million
4. Page 14 18 bones
   25 − 7 = 18

Glossary

adapt | (uh-DAPT) to adjust to a new set of circumstances (page 15)

adaptation | (a-dap-TAY-shun) a change in structure, function, or form that aids in survival (page 19)

arthropod | (AR-thruh-pod) an invertebrate with jointed legs, a segmented body, and an exoskeleton (page 7)

camouflage | (KA-muh-flahj) coloring that allows an animal to blend in with its surroundings (page 22)

chordate | (KOR-date) an animal having a dorsal nerve running down the middle of its back (page 7)

class | (KLAS) a classification category between phylum and order (page 9)

classification | (kla-sih-fih-KAY-shun) the process of separating organisms with similar characteristics (page 4)

exoskeleton | (ek-soh-SKEH-leh-tun) a hard, external, support structure (page 7)

family | (FA-mih-lee) the classification group immediately above genus (page 10)

genus | (JEE-nus) one of the original two classification categories (page 10)

invertebrate | (in-VER-teh-brut) an animal without a backbone (page 8)

kingdom | (KING-dum) the largest grouping in the classification system used by taxonomists (page 6)

order | (OR-der) the classification category below class and above family (page 9)

phylum | (FY-lum) the classification category below kingdom; singular form of *phyla* (page 7)

species | (SPEE-sheez) one of the original two classification categories (page 10)

trait | (TRAYT) a distinguishing quality or characteristic (page 4)

vertebrate | (VER-teh-brut) an animal with a bony spinal column (page 8)

Index